INTERVIEW FITNESS TRAINING

A Workout With Carole Martin

THE INTERVIEW COACH

Interview Publishing
1-877-647-5627
www.InterviewCoach.com

3rd Edition

ISBN 0-9709012-0-8
ISBN 0-9709012-1-6
ISBN 0-9709012-2-4

INTRODUCTION

As with any workout/fitness training you must make a commitment in order to improve your skills. The exercises in this book will be more effective if you are willing to put in time and energy and take an active part in the process - to build up your interview muscles.

The interview is a type of performance, or presentation. You will need to do some preparation and have a rehearsal. You will need to put effort into your exercises to become a stronger presenter. The goal is to be prepared and natural.

If, after doing the exercises, you would like to practice with a professional, I will welcome the opportunity to work with you. If you have any questions regarding the exercises or book content you can contact me by email at Carole@InterviewCoach.com or call me toll-free at 1-877-647-5627.

This workbook will

help you
- focus on your strengths and what you have to offer a company.
- prepare your success stories to answer those difficult behavioral questions "Tell me about a time...."
- script your answers to difficult questions.
- have a stronger impact on others.

give you
- more power in the interview process.
- more confidence and a feeling of being prepared.
- methods to answer questions effectively.
- the mind-set to be more selective and in control.
- skills to negotiate a better offer.
- permission to not get an offer after every interview.

Now, let the workout begin!

TESTIMONIALS - WHAT PEOPLE ARE SAYING

Jennifer Robin, Image Consultant
Author of Clothe Your Spirit
Carole Martin's positive approach makes the interview process seem like fun. She has a special gift for making each reader feel worthwhile. Her book is utterly professional and very helpful."

Reviewer Kim Draper, BookReviewClub.com
The night before the interview we all have the same feeling in the pit of our stomachs, dread. Yes, that is the word for it. No need to have all those feeling anymore, Carole Martin has written a wonderful book on learning how to trample the interviewing anxiety bug. This is a very in-depth book that can teach you how to breeze through a job interview with flying colors. She teaches you how to release our anxieties, relaxation tips, and how to learn from your past interview mistakes. But Ms. Martin does not stop there. She actually teaches you how to market the product, and that product happens to be you. You are the product, and you are trying to sell yourself to the interviewer so they will hire you.

This is one book that all of us need to read at least once. She has valuable tips and question and answers sections for the beginner to the novice interviewee. Take the time to read this one today, you never know when you might need it.

Reviewer Warren Thurston, eBook Reviews Weekly
All people seeking employment can learn how to improve their interview skills. Techniques are available that will help to improve their prospects of getting jobs. Carole Martin's book is an excellent source to guide people in the right direction.

A reader from Springfield, NC
Carole Martin has a special gift for making each reader feel worthwhile. Her book is utterly professional and very helpful.

A reader from Colorado Springs, CO
I've been through many interviews. This workbook hits all of the important points, reviews the obvious and gives new tips and ideas to help get the job. I've aced my interview because I followed Ms. Martin's advice. I like her real-life scenarios and humor. I highly recommend the book.

A reader from Carlisle, PA
Takes the guesswork out of interviewing process. I have always been afraid of interviews, but now I have no doubt I can get the job I want! Made me completely confident in myself, I may surprise a lot of interviewers now that I know what they expect. Great book!

Thank you from San Diego, CA
I just returned from an interview with the federal government and can't thank you enough for all your help. I purchased the manual three days before as a "last attempt" to feel secure, and it really put me at ease about the whole situation...how to relieve that fear, prepare, etc. I nailed it!

New VP Jeff B.
I met Carole after reading an article in which she was interviewed. I did some due diligence and was comfortable working with her after verifying her media credentials. I was able to see that she has been an authority on interviewing for many reporters and journalists. When I initially contacted her, she spoke with me at great length about my situation without any money or commitment on my part. This made me very comfortable. She sent me several emails with worksheets to prepare for our mock interview. The exercises were extremely helpful. I then had a one-hour session with her via telephone where she interviewed me, and we listened to it and critiqued it.

I have never been concerned about an interview, but this position was for more money than I had ever earned before, so I was a bit nervous. After our session, I asked Carole if we should get together again before the interview to make sure I had really nailed down my responses. She said that it was not necessary and that I was plenty ready for this interview. That made me very confident, knowing that she could have easily billed me for another hour, but instead she said I was ready. I flew out three days later for my interview and heard back one week later that I not only got the job, but also the territory they had previously insinuated I probably wouldn't get, plus a signing bonus that was not previously on the table. Seeing they had upped the ante beyond the originally discussed salary without being asked, I decided to counter their offer, and they responded with even more money in less than a day.

I highly recommend Carole to anyone who wants to greatly improve their chances at landing a new position.

TABLE OF CONTENTS

* Indicates Interview Exercise

INTERVIEW ANXIETY

EVERYBODY GETS NERVOUS

It's OK To Be Nervous

It would be nice if your heart didn't palpitate, and your hands didn't sweat, and your mouth didn't go dry, but most people, even executives, experience one or more of these symptoms when they interview. But here's the good news: it's OK to be nervous. Let me repeat that. It's OK to be nervous, and it is essential for you to accept the way you feel.

It is very unrealistic to tell yourself you should be different from the way you really are. It just makes you feel worse about yourself. By shifting your thinking to self-acceptance, you feel more in control and more confident almost immediately.

What's the Worst Thing That Can Happen?

For many people the worst thing that can happen is "rejection" - not getting an offer. It is a common fear. Who wants to be rejected? It's much more desirable to be the "rejecter," the one to say, "No thank you. I don't think I'll take your job offer." Did you ever think that maybe that job wasn't right for you? that maybe you weren't being objective about the process? that you just wanted an offer - to be accepted? Try to look at the process from another perspective: as a learning experience.

Face the Fear

What is making you feel nervous? What is it you fear? If one of our greatest fears is rejection, and one of our greatest needs is acceptance, going through the interview process is like walking on hot coals.

According to author Susan Jeffers, Phd. (<u>Feel the Fear and Do It Anyway</u>),

"The only way to get rid of the fear of doing something is to go out... and do it."

"The only way to feel better about myself is to go out... and do it."

Some things are out of your control - don't take them personally.

 An Interviewer's Story

Conducting interviews for an accountant position, and working with the accounting manager, I found a woman I thought was a wonderful match for the position. I sent her forward to meet the manager.

The manager contacted me later that day. I inquired about the candidate. She replied, "I liked her." She then said, "But I'm not going to hire her!" I was taken aback. "Why not?" I asked.

"Because she looks exactly like my aunt. And I hate my aunt. And I could not come in here every day and look at her face!"

That candidate was rejected, not because of anything she did or didn't do, but because of a strange circumstance.

WHAT PAST INTERVIEW EXPERIENCES CAN YOU LEARN FROM?

Facing the Fear

"Last time I wasn't prepared, and I just tried to wing it. This time I'm going to get my act together and prepare and practice."

"I was caught off-guard when I was asked what I was looking for in the way of a salary. This time I've done my research and homework, and I'm going to be prepared."

 EXERCISE

Releasing Anxiety - Name Those Fears

Spend some time thinking about and identifying your anxiety. Write down your issues, or answer the questions below. Write anything else that makes you nervous. By looking at what is making you feel anxious, you can begin to deal with the "monster" and begin to practice accepting your feelings or changing your thinking.

What do you fear most about the interview?

What's the worst thing that can happen?

What questions do you fear?

What are your biggest stumbling blocks?
Difficult questions?

Have you had past successes with interviews? What went right?

What didn't go so well?

What do you want the interviewer to know about you?
Your strengths?

What do you want to soften or avoid?

Are you concerned only about the end result of the interview
or are you checking out the company as well?

RELAXATION TIPS

Breathing

Relaxation needs to be practiced long before you enter the interview. Try this easy breathing technique to relax.

Breathe in through your nose, filling your stomach with air. Hold for a few seconds and then exhale through your mouth, making a swooshing sound. Repeat again and again until it becomes a natural response to release tension.

Practice this anytime you want to let go and relax or are feeling tense. You could even do it in a quiet manner while waiting for your interviewer.

Yoga, meditation, and relaxation therapy are other great ways to learn how to relax and gain control.

*Our greatest fear is that we will
not be able to cope.
It's OK not to get an offer.*

Damp Hands

The interview almost always begins with a handshake. "Hello, I am Susan Cook," says the interviewer, and she extends her hand. It is now your turn to extend your hand in return. But your palm is damp.

Should you:

    A. Quickly wipe your hand on the side of your pants or skirt?

    B. Stick out your damp hand?

    C. Keep your hand to yourself?

None of the above is very desirable.

Try These Tips:

1. Arrive at the interview 10-15 minutes early (always a good idea - NEVER LATE!).

2. Go to the rest room and run cold water on the insides of your wrists for a few minutes, and breathe - relax. In the case of cold hands, try running hot water to warm your hands. The insides of your wrists are very temperature sensitive. This remedy can last up to half an hour. Try it and see if it works for you.

3. Anti-perspirant gel deoderant can be used like a hand lotion on your palms. People have reported that their hands stay dry, soft, and smell good. (Try this tip before the interview day to see if it works on your hands.)

Firm Handshake

It is important that your grip demonstrates confidence. A firm handshake, not a bone-crushing grip, will indicate self-assurance. Reach your hand out palm sideways and grip the hand, web to web. Try it, you will see that your hand closes over the palm of the hand. When you squeeze the fingers, it can hurt, especially if you are wearing rings.

Seven Steps Toward Making a Good Impression

1. Appearance counts. When you look good, you feel good. Make sure you look groomed and neat. Check odors (good and bad). Too much cologne or perfume can be a real turn-off.

2. Your clothes and accessories should be conservative and neutral. Your clothes are your packaging and should not take attention away from you as the product.

3. Non-verbal communication sometimes conveys a stronger message than verbal communication. Sit or stand up straight (like your mother always told you).

4. Eye contact and smiles can indicate a confident and upbeat attitude. This is a good opportunity to demonstrate your social and interpersonal skills.

5. The handshake sends a strong tactile message. Your grip should be firm (show some sign of life - even men with women) - but not bone-crushing.

6. Your voice and the volume of your speech convey a strong impression. Whether it is a phone interview or a face-to-face interview, it is important that you speak with enthusiasm and energy.

7. Your vocabulary reveals your communication skills and ability to interface with people, especially people you've not met before.

When you get off on the right foot, the interview will flow easily. This is one impression you cannot leave to chance.

THE INTERVIEW AS A TWO-WAY PROCESS

A Conversation

Begin to think of the interview as a conversation - a conversation with a purpose. The conversation should be two-way and interactive.

Instead of focusing on the end result, you need to learn to listen.

Missing Out on a Great Opportunity

What parts of your body are not used effectively in the job interview?

If you said, "Your ears," you are correct. Most people fail to "hear" what is going on in the interview.

If you think interviewing is only about answering questions, you've been missing the point. You've also been missing an opportunity to gather valuable information. Most people go into the interview thinking and worrying about how they will answer the questions, and they forget that they are there to find out about the job and the company. They forget to listen, observe, and read between the lines.

Here are some benefits you receive by improving on your listening techniques.

· You hear where the emphasis is placed by the questions asked and general talk about the company.
· You begin to pick up clues from the conversation, and you can ask questions and ask for clarification.
· Listening carefully and reading between the lines will help you in your decision of whether or not you want to work for this company, in this department.

When all you can think of is the answer that you will be giving, you miss a premium opportunity to garner information about the situation you are about to enter. Turn up your listening and intuitive skills. Read between the lines! You'll be surprised by what you hear.

You are interviewing them as much as they are interviewing you!

"I always thought of myself as a goalie at a hockey game when I interviewed. My job was to return those pucks - to be like the defense." Jim - Public Defender.

Wrong, Jim!

Your job is to listen and ask questions and to send some of those pucks their way. Find out if this is a good place for you.

 True Story

A young woman walked into an interview with an older man. He indicated to her that she should sit across from him at the desk.

He then proceeded to tilt his chair all the way back and put his hands behind his head (a very intimidating posture). He asked her, "So, why do you want to work for my company?"

She leaned forward in her chair and said, "Well, that's why I'm here today - to find out if this would be a good place for me to work."

The man sat up straight in his chair, looked her in the eye, and the interview continued, as professionals having a conversation.

INTERVIEWING WITH A CONSULTANT MIND-SET

Tell Me About Your Problem

Interviewing with a "consultant" mind-set can help you. Take the time to analyze what the company is seeking, not just what is written in the ad posting or job description, but what it will take to get the job done, and done well!

Consultants listen and analyze the problem. They think of possible solutions to the problem.

Listening is the key. Most people like to talk and don't really listen well. Listen to what the interviewer(s) talk about, what is asked and what comments are made. Does the conversation revolve around the employees, the employees' work, the customer? This should give you clues as to what is the most important product and the company's values. What are the issues/problems? Do they have a mission statement? Is the statement relevant? Do you hear evidence of the mission being supported by the work?

Some interviewers will tell you more than others. Sometimes you have to read between the lines - not everything will be said. Use your intuition!

It is important for you to prepare questions to ask them.

see page 66

True Story

The applicant was interviewed for 90 minutes by two interviewers. At the end of the interview, the interviewers asked if she had any questions. "Yes," she replied. "On a scale of one to ten, where does morale stand in this company?"

The interviewers looked at one other and replied, "A seven."

"So, there are some issues?" she asked.

"Yes," replied the interviewers.

"From the questions you asked me, it sounds like you two are very overwhelmed and need someone to come in and hit the ground running, right?" she asked.

"Yes," they replied in unison, "At last someone understands our problem."

"I can tell you that I have been there and done that, and there wasn't anything you said today that I haven't experienced before. I think I can make a difference from the beginning if you hire me," she said.

She got the job! She had listened to the problem and let the interviewers know that she understood the problem and was ready to be the solution. It was a win/win situation for everyone.

The Equation:

Employer has a problem - work to get done, issues to deal with, problems to solve.

You may be the answer to the problem - you have the skills, background, experience, and attitude.

Challenge: to convince the employer that you can bring added value to the equation, to help with the problem.

Solution: A win/win for everyone.

$$\frac{\text{EMPLOYER} + \text{YOU} - \text{CHALLENGE}}{\text{WIN/WIN}}$$

*Sell yourself as
the solution to the problem.*

THE PRODUCT - YOU

What Do You Have to Offer?

Most people say they feel really uncomfortable bragging about themselves. That figures, because we have been told since we were children, "Don't brag." But the job interview is not the place to become modest about your achievements. It is, in fact, the place to talk about them with pride.

Myth - "The Best-Qualified Candidate Always Gets The Job!"

You have to create the perception that you are the best candidate. Saying "The best-qualified candidate always gets the job," is like saying "The best product always captures the market." This is not always the case. Not only must the product be the best, but it must be perceived to be the best. Perception is the key. If you are best qualified but not perceived to be best, you may lose your opportunity. Let the interviewer know you are the best qualified! If you can talk about your skills in a convincing manner, you are the one most likely to get the job.

A change of focus will help a lot in this area. Begin to think of yourself as a PRODUCT! When you are considering buying a product, you want to know what it has to offer. What do you have to offer?

One way to think about your skills is to divide them into three categories:

1. Knowledge-based Skills. Many employers hire based on knowledge-based skills alone. In fact, there are some employers who are willing to hire sight-unseen over the phone. "If you have the right background, we'll hire you." BEWARE! There is more to the job than the duties. Culture, personality fit, chemistry - all are a part of your job satisfaction in a company.

2. Transferable or Portable Skills. Identifying transferable skills is especially important for anyone who is transferring to another field or type of organization. Think about what you have to offer in the way of transferable skills - organizational skills, management/business skills, research or teaching skills, analytical or problem-solving skills. Chances are that you are taking for granted some of the skills that make you unique.

3. Personal Skills or Traits – These are skills that cannot be taught by an employer. These are inherent traits and habits developed and learned over time. Because of the ever-changing world we live in, flexibility and adaptability are becoming among the most desirable personal traits.

Once you identify your skills and your strengths, you can begin to build your resume and interviewing preparation around these skills to market and sell yourself. By listing your skills, you will also be preparing for your "Tell Me About Yourself" statement on page 48.

Standing Out From the Other Candidates

"How can you make yourself stand out when there are so many other candidates looking at the same job?" The answer is "focus" - focus on what makes you unique.

Let's assume that you have an outstanding resume and that you make it to the top of the stack of resumes of people to be called for an interview. You, and maybe nine or ten other equally qualified people for the position, that is.

Because companies have so many candidates to choose from, they are interviewing more people so that they can select the "best." When you are lucky enough to be invited to an interview, it is essential that you be ready to sell yourself, to let the interviewers know what makes you unique, what added value you can bring to the position. In other words, tell why you are the best person for the job.

By doing some basic preparation, you can determine your uniqueness and where you should focus your attention. The first step in this process is to identify your five strengths. These strengths are the areas where you do very well.

Identifying Your Five Strengths

This may take some thought on your part. What are your strengths? Think about previous performance appraisals. What was said or written about you? What would your co-workers or ex-bosses say about you?

- List the skills and experiences you have that would be required in the type of job you are seeking. For instance, a technical job would focus on programs, languages, platforms, etc.

- Give some thought to those skills in which you excel, those that are referred to as the "soft skills." These skills can be viewed as transferable: You can take them with you to any job you hold. Examples of these skills are your communication and people skills, or your time-management and project-management skills, or your ability to build strong relationships, or your ability to influence others.

- Lastly, think of the personal traits that make you unique. Maybe you never miss deadlines, or perhaps you are willing to do above and beyond what is asked, or perhaps you have a great attitude. (Don't dismiss these traits--many people have been fired for negative personal traits rather than for lack of knowledge).

When you have identified your five strengths, make a list of those strengths and some examples of when those strengths have helped you achieve results on the job. It will be essential that you can not only identify your strengths, but that you also have examples and stories of times when you demonstrated those strengths in the past.

The next step is to look at the job postings and ads. In fact, look at several job postings that would be of interest to you. Your goal is to find key words and phrases. For this exercise, don't limit yourself to geographical location. Look at jobs of interest located anywhere.

When you have several postings, read each word and sentence carefully, taking notes as you do. What are they looking for? What words appear consistently in almost every posting?

In summary, by narrowing your uniqueness to five basic points, you can guide the conversation to include this information. By focusing on five strengths, you will be prepared with examples of times when you have used these strengths.

When you walk out of that interview room, your interviewers may not remember all five of your points; but if they remember even two of the points that make you unique, you will be ahead of the game!

WHAT MAKES YOU UNIQUE?

Think about and write down the skills you have used in past jobs (only the ones you want to use in your next job). Name at least seven to ten in each category. What do you have to offer from your last job? from your previous jobs? from your education? from your volunteer work? from your life experiences?

Identify Your Knowledge-Based Skills – skills you learned from experience and education.
(Analyzing, Estimating, Coordinating, Negotiating, Organizing, Public Speaking, Mechanically Adept, Leadership, Counseling, Artistic, Computer Skills, Entrepreneurial, Design, Budgeting, Training, Project Management)

List Your Transferable or Portable Skills – skills that will work in different industries and jobs.
(Communication, Planning, Time Management, Problem Solving, Customer Service, Teaching, Coaching, Creative, Researching, Selling, Follow-through, Resourcefulness, Attention to detail, Skilled with numbers, Innovation)

Think About Your Personal Traits – the qualities that make you who you are.
(Flexible, Friendly, Dependable, Good Attitude, Reliable, Calm, High Energy, Patient, Self-starter, Organized, Easy to Get Along With, Quick Learner, People Skills, Goal Directed)

MOTIVATION

What Are You Looking For?

It is important that you think about what you want. Think about when you have been most satisfied with your career. Also think about when you have been least satisfied? Was your last job satisfying? What would you have liked more of? Less of? Take the time to give this exercise some thought. It could make a difference in your job satisfaction. How can you find the right job if you don't know what you are looking for? Hopefully, we learn from our past experiences – positive and negative.

Q. When have you been most satisfied with your career? Why?

A. "That would have to be my last job where I..."
"The reason I was satisfied is because I was doing..."

EXERCISE

WHAT MOTIVATES YOU?

Think about the various jobs you've held. Which were the best remembered? Which were those you would just as soon forget? If you can't think of jobs, think about projects. If you are a new grad, think of classes you've taken which have been of particular interest.

Answer the questions on the next page.

1. When have you been most productive, energized, and content with your work?

Why?

How can you look for this in your next job? What questions can you ask to try to discern whether this is the place for you?

2. When have you been least satisfied? Miserable? Unhappy? Hated going to work?

Why?

What questions could you ask in the interview to try to find out more about the culture and the work environment at the company you are interviewing with? How can you avoid getting into a similar situation again?

Matching Your Qualifications With Their Needs

When you read the ads/postings carefully, you will notice that there are some words included in every ad for your type of job. An example would be ads for an Executive Secretary where the word "confidentiality" appears consistently. If you were to apply for that particular position, you would want to be sure to include the word "confidentiality" in your resume and cover letter.

Read job postings carefully looking for the words that are repeated or stand out as being the most important factors to perform the job. These words are called the "key factors" or the key competencies required to do the job.

By practicing to identify key factors in job postings or ads that are of interest, you will begin to notice patterns. What are the common words used in almost every description? What are they looking for? What qualifications are listed? How do your skills match up against their requirements?

A good exercise is to take a piece of paper and write down the words that appear repeatedly. Notice the frequency of particular words. These "key factors" for the type of jobs that you are applying will become pertinent to your preparation for the interview. These words will also be an indicator to the interviewer that you know the "lingo." If they use industry words, you should include those words.

FIT? THEIR NEEDS - YOUR QUALITIES

Take a job description (a classified ad or job posting will work as well). Looking at the job description, compare the company's needs with your experience and qualities. How do you stack up? Where are your shortcomings? Can you show how you learn quickly or bring added value to the company from the start? Write some ideas in the following columns:

What Are They Looking For?
(Key Factors)

WHAT I HAVE TO OFFER
(What makes you unique?)

Do you have other qualities that will replace those required -
years of experience vs. education? Do you fit at least 80% of
the requirements?

The Words You Use Send a Strong Message

The words you use to express yourself say more about you than you think. In fact, your vocabulary and the use of appropriate words say more about you than the message you are trying communicate. You are judged by the words you use. When you are looking for a job it is not only important to use the "right" words and language - it is essential.

It begins with the writing of your resume and continues in the way that you answer the questions asked in an interview. Each industry uses "key words" or "lingo" for each position. In order to be prepared, it will be important for you to research these words and to use them appropriately. If you do, you will sound more knowledgeable and "in-the-know."

How will I know which words are "key"?

Key words are found in job postings/ads. For each position there are common words that describe what is required for a job. Job postings are a list of qualities and skills employers are looking for in a candidate, their "wish list."

Here is an example of common words used in postings for an Executive Secretary position: (Six postings were used).

- "Confidential" (used in all six postings)
- "Ability to proofread and edit" (used in all six postings)
- "Excellent written and verbal communication skills" (used in four of six postings)
- "Organized, Attention to detail" (used in all six postings)
- Other words used included, "Discretion," Judgment," Self-starter," Scheduling," "Prioritize," and "Multi-tasking."

If you are applying for an Executive secretary position, these are the key words to include in your cover letter and resume. Electronic resume scanners will seek out these words to select your resume as qualified for the position. If these words are missing, your resume may not be selected. These are also the words to use in the interview that will make you sound like someone who is a good fit for the position.

The right words can make a big difference in a single statement: more concise and to the point, more powerful and impressive. Finding the "key" words will make your statements more powerful. Speaking the industry lingo, you will be taken more seriously as a candidate worthy of a job offer

BEHAVIORAL INTERVIEWING
PAST BEHAVIOR = FUTURE SUCCESS

You Say You're Good - Prove It!

Skilled interviewers use behavioral interviewing techniques to screen out candidates. But what does that mean?

In order to find experienced people, employers are asking interview questions based on past behavior as an indicator of future success. In other words, if you can demonstrate through examples, especially recent examples, that you've had success in certain areas at a previous time, you will be looked upon as a possible candidate for success in a future position.

Past behavior is an indicator of future success - if you did it before you can do it again - good or bad.

The questions asked in behavioral interviewing are different from traditional interview questions. A traditional question might begin with a statement like, "What would you do if..." You can use your imagination with that type of question and spin a tale.

Not so with behavior-based interviewing. An example of a behavioral question would be, "Tell me about a time when...," or "Can you give me an example...." The interviewer is looking for specific examples of how you handled situations.

Your tendency when asked a question like this might be to say, "I do that every day - it's what I do." But the interviewer using behavioral interviewing is looking for specific examples of how you performed. The interviewer might say, "Can you give me an example of a time when you handled a dissatisfied customer?" It is now time for you to tell your success story. Your stories should include the situation, what you did, the action you took, and the result or outcome.

Employers are looking for employees who have experience and skills. They are listening for examples of past successes and how you handled failures. Your examples will demonstrate your experience with people, your flexibility, and your willingness to grow with the job.

If the interviewer does not use this interviewing technique, you can still tell your stories when appropriate. As an example, you could say, "I'd like to tell you about my customer service experience that I think would be important in this job."

By preparing for the interview with an exercise recalling your past stories, you will be able to think of examples ahead of time and not be caught off-guard. There is nothing worse than going home after an interview thinking of all the things you could have said. Your stories don't necessarily have to be about paid work. Examples of volunteering, community work, or your education can also be effective. Try to make the examples specific to the type of position you are applying for, and be sure the stories are true stories. This is no time for fairy tales.

You say you're a hard worker.
Prove it.
Give me an example.

YOUR SUCCESS STORIES

Telling the Whole Story

Writing your success stories is the most important step toward interview preparation. The first step of this process is to determine which factors are crucial to the position for which you are applying. Look at a job description or a classified ad, such as the one below, and determine what it would take to get the job done.

What crucial factors would you be looking for if you were recruiting for this job? What skills and traits would it take for success in this position?

> **WANTED: Customer Service Representative**
> Seeking a self-motivated individual with professional communication skills. Must have customer service experience with the ability to work with internal and external customers using good listening skills. Knowledge of the Internet and MS office products is a must.

Some key words in this ad that you may have identified are:

- Communication skills
- Professional attitude
- Listening skills
- Self-Motivated
- Customer Service experience
- Computer skills.

The next step is to write experience stories around these factors. One of the easiest ways to prepare and remember stories is to use an acronym - **SPARE**. It's a lot like writing a story with a beginning, a middle, and an end.

Situation, or **P**roblem. What is the basis of the story? State the situation or problem at the beginning of your story. It should be brief and concise. What was the situation?

Action. What you did, your actions. (Beware of the pronoun we. It can take away from your part of the action). This part of the story should include some movement and detail.

Results. What was the outcome or ending to the story? (The end is an important part of the story, which a lot of people neglect to add.) The story does not always have to end in a success. Overcoming adversity and beginning again is also a trait that employers are looking for in a candidate.

Enthusiasm. Tell the story in an interesting way, adding details that bring color and interest to the story as though you were telling it to someone at a party (in professional language).

Using a Success Story

An interviewer looking for a Customer Service Representative may ask a question like, "Describe a situation when you had to handle an angry customer and make a quick decision about the action taken."

This would be your chance to tell one of your prepared success stories.

Situation or Problem

"I can remember a woman who called and was yelling about a malfunction of a machine that had cost her an order."

Action

"First, I listened very carefully; then I calmed her down by asking her to explain the details of the situation. I then repeated the problem back to her and confirmed that I understood the problem. I assured her I would call her back that day. I did some research on the problem and the dates and discussed the situation with my supervisor. I recommended that we adjust the customer's bill based on my findings, and my supervisor agreed."

Result

"I called her back that day, as promised, and she was very satisfied with the adjustment. She even wrote an Email to my supervisor telling him about my excellent and professional customer service."

Enthusiasm

"I really liked solving her problem. I felt like I had done something worthwhile when she thanked me and apologized for chewing me out."

What traits can you pick up from the story?

• good customer service
• communications skills
• listening skills
• follow-through
• initiative
• research skills
• problem-solving

If you were recruiting for this position, would you be interested in this person?

WRITING YOUR OWN SUCCESS STORIES - SPARE

EXERCISE

Look at the job description or ad posting for the position you are seeking, and select the key factors - what it would take to get the job done. Using the SPARE format, write at least 5-10 stories about each factor identified. Focus on the factors they are seeking and show them you have what it takes because you have done it before.

STORY TEMPLATE

Situation or **P**roblem (20%)

Action (60%)

Result (20%)

Enthusiasm (+)

THE PREPARATION

"TELL ME ABOUT YOURSELF"

Where Do I Begin? Where Should I Focus?

The #1 question asked in most interviews is "TELL ME ABOUT YOURSELF" or some form of that question. "How would you describe yourself?" or "Tell me about yourself and your background and how it relates to this position."

Beginning. Tell about your years of work experience - your most recent work, skills, and achievements - some of your knowledge-based skills and how you used them.

Transition. Emphasize your transferable skills, your strengths. What do you have to offer? What can you bring to this position? What are your accomplishments?

Current Situation. Describe what you're looking for now. What type of work have you enjoyed? What qualities have motivated you before and are you hoping to find again?

EXAMPLE #1:

Beginning:
For the past six years, I have been in the electronics industry working on computer systems. Two years ago I was promoted to lead technician and currently supervise four testers and technicians.

Transition:
My strength is problem solving. I take an analytical view of what is happening and work through the process by trying various solutions. I work well independently or as a member of a team. I have worked in fast-paced environments most of my life, and I am very goal-oriented and deadline-driven.

Current Situation:
I am looking for a position as a lead or coach where I can effectively work with a team to bring in results that contribute to the bigger picture or bottom line.

EXAMPLE #2:

Beginning:
I am a person who enjoys problem solving. For the past six years I have been working on projects and problems involving software design. In my last position I was able to solve a design problem that had been around for more than a year. As a result, the company was able to sell a product that had been delayed for a key account of over $2 million.

Transition:
I enjoy thinking "outside of the box" and coming up with new ways to look at old problems, either on my own or as a team member. Customer service and follow-through are skills I pride myself on. I have made some long-lasting relationships with customers by building rapport through trust. I pride myself on making people feel special, no matter what size the account.

Current Situation:
It is important to me to do work that makes a difference, no matter what my role. I am looking for new challenges in the software industry. I'd like to find a place where I can bring what I have learned and apply it to new situations.

This is your personal statement that you will use over and over while in search of a job.

EXERCISE

YOUR PERSONAL STATEMENT

Prepare a brief but concise statement that would take two minutes or less to say as a response to the "Tell me about yourself" question. This is the oral version of a summary you might use on a resume.

Beginning - (experience - overall/recent)
Three sentences

Transition - (highlight your strengths)
Two sentences

Current Situation - (present - looking for now)

IMPORTANT:

Practice this statement until it sounds smooth, not stilted or rehearsed. Use a tape recorder or a coach to practice, practice, practice.

PREPARE FOR SALARY QUESTIONS
Don't be caught off-guard!

Know the Market - Know Your Worth

"Could you tell me what salary you are looking for?"

"What are you currently making?"

"Your salary need is clearly out of our range. Are you still interested in pursuing the position?"

"Would you be willing to consider a cut in pay?"

Questions concerning compensation can be asked as early as a phone screening. A part of your preparation should include some work on how to answer the questions regarding salary before the interview even begins.

The rule here is, "Delay the subject of salary as long as possible." If you name a number this early in the process, you will set the line for future negotiations.

Tell your interviewer that you feel it is premature to discuss the subject of money until you have more information about the position and the responsibilities involved. Ask him or her, "Could you tell me the range budgeted for this position?"

Research

It is important that you do your homework before you go into the interview. YOU MUST KNOW YOUR WORTH.

- What is the going rate for the position?
- Compare like positions, years of experience, responsibilities, region.
- Check out Web sites, associations, colleagues.

Think about buying a major purchase, like a car. What research process would you go through? Blue book? Check the classifieds to find out the going rate for the model and year? Check with mechanics? Read Consumers Report?

The same process applies to researching the job and salary. Take some time before you go out to buy.

Web sites with salary information:

http://www.salary.com
http://www.jobstar.org
http://www.salaryexpert.com
http://www.wageweb.com

For more Web site resources sites see Page 101

Know Your Bottom Line

What is the lowest salary you are willing to accept (no matter how terrific the job!)? Do some calculations. Figure out what you want and what you need to maintain your current lifestyle or to improve your current lifestyle. Know when you have to say, "No, I can't accept the offer at that salary." See exercise "Figuring Your Bottom Line" on the next page.

 An Interviewer's Story

A client of mine was interviewing for a position in the high tech industry. When he was interviewed by the CEO, he was asked, "What do you want in the way of salary?" His interviewer told him it was not his policy to play games about salary.

The man answered, "Somewhere between $50,000 and $60,000."

He called me to say he had received an offer from the company for $60,000. "Good for you!" I exclaimed. He said, "No, I did some research and found out with my credentials and experience I am worth $70,000."

"So why did you say $50 to 60 thousand?" I asked.

"Because they caught me off-guard," came his reply.

EXERCISE

FIGURING YOUR BOTTOM LINE
What Do You Need to Keep Up Your Current Lifestyle?
To Improve Your Lifestyle?

	NEED	WANT
Fixed Monthly Expenses		
Rent/Mortgage Expense		
Utilities (Gas, Electric, Water)		
Telephone		
Insurance (Medical, Life, Home, Auto)		
Loan Payments		
Credit Card Payments		
Cellular Phone Bill		
Internet Provider		
Other		
Other		
Fixed Monthly Total		

	NEED	WANT
Variable Fixed Expenses		
Transportation		
Food		
Clothing		
Personal/Household Items		
Entertainment Expenses/Recreation		
Travel/Vacations		
Education		
Professional Memberships/dues/meetings		
Savings/Investments		
Medical/Dental Care		
Taxes		
Charitable Donations		
Gifts		
Other		
Variable Fixed Total		
Fixed Monthly Total (from previous page)		
WHAT YOU NEED/WANT TO EARN		

HOW TO DEAL WITH DIFFICULT QUESTIONS

The Most Dreaded Question of All

There is a formula for difficult questions called the Sandwich Technique.

(+) Begin with a positive statement
(-) Slip in the negative (or weakness)
(+) End with a positive statement

Q: WHAT ARE YOUR GREATEST STRENGTHS
AND WEAKNESSES?

A: (+) My strengths are my energy and enthusiasm. I have a proven track record for working above and beyond what is asked of me.

(-) My weakness is that I get impatient when I don't get the data I need to do my job because someone else didn't meet a deadline.

(+) I continue to work on stronger communication skills so that I can deal with and understand people who don't have the same work ethic.

This answer works because we can all work on our communication skills, particularly when it comes to being understanding of someone who is not pulling his/her weight. This is not the time to reveal a time-management or planning problem. Think of something you would like to improve about yourself. Be careful of sounding like a workaholic or a perfectionist – and always have a story ready (SPARE - page 44) to back up your statements.

ANSWER WITH A SANDWICH

What is your greatest strength/weakness? Practice writing out your answer - be sure to sandwich the negative with an emphasis on the positive.

(+)

(-)

(+)

Dear Interview Coach

An Email was received that read:
Dear Interview Coach,
I don't know what to say when asked, "What are your weaknesses?" I don't have any weaknesses.

The reply:
Dear God,
We all have weaknesses!

EXERCISE

ANSWERS TO STANDARD QUESTIONS

Inevitably, there are some standard questions that come up in almost every interview. Think about how you would answer these questions and practice your answers. Even if you aren't asked these specific questions, it will be good practice for you to think about this information. You may be able to use the information to answer another question. Use the page numbers provided to research your answers.

"Tell me about yourself." (page 48)

"Why did you leave (are you leaving) your last company?"
(page 56)

"What is your salary expectation?" (pages 52 and 54)

"When have you been most satisfied in your career?"
(page 32)

"When have you been most dissatisfied in your career?"
(page 32)

"What is your greatest strength?" (page 30)

"What is your greatest weakness?" (page 56)

"What experience do you have that qualifies you for this position?" (page 50)

"What attracted you to this position and/or company?" (pages 32 and 36)

"When have you been most motivated?" (page 32)

"Tell me about a time when you had a disagreement/confrontation with a boss/coworker." (pages 42 and 45)

"Tell me about the most difficult assignment you've ever had." (pages 42 and 45)

"Why should we hire you?" (pages 30 and 50)

"Why do you want to work for this company?" (page 20)

"Tell me about a time when you had to adapt to a change quickly." (pages 42 and 45)

"Can you give me an example of working in a fast-paced environment?" (pages 42 and 45)

"On your resume you say you are a 'hard worker'. Can you give me an example of hard work?" (pages 42 and 45)

"Do you have any questions?" (page 66)

FREQUENT INTERVIEW CONCERNS

What is an Illegal Question?

- How old are you?
- Do you have children?
- How is your health?
- Are you a U.S. citizen?
- Have you ever been arrested?

Illegal or improper? That is the question.

Technically, it is illegal for an interviewer to ask anything personal that is not directly job-related. Off-limit questions include, but are not limited to: information regarding your age, marital status, country of origin, religion, sexual orientation, and health status. Almost any legal information about you is illegal in the job interview.

Example
The female candidate was asked, "Do you plan to have children?" She was taken aback by the question and wasn't sure how to answer.

She had three choices:

A. To answer the question honestly even though she did not want to.

B. To tell the interviewer it is none of his business and the question is illegal.

C. To deal with the concern behind the question, ignoring the illegal question itself.

How would you answer the question if you were the female candidate?

The best answer is "C."

An appropriate answer from the candidate might have been, "Whether or not I plan to have children in the future is not really relevant to my career. I plan to work and have a career no matter what happens in my personal life."

Why is this type of question asked in an interview? Why are interviewers concerned about your plans to reproduce, your marital status and your retirement plans? It's simple; they want to make sure you are the solution to a problem, not the source of more headaches.

When the female candidate was asked her plans regarding future motherhood, the interviewer may have been trying to determine whether she was in for the long-term or just until the company could pay for the birth of her firstborn. It is clearly a discriminatory question, one that would probably never be asked of a male candidate, and it is illegal!

When you are asked this type of question, consider that you have options as to how you will answer.

1. You can answer the question and move on. (This may not feel good, but how important is the question to you?)

2. Don't answer the questions when asked. (This may feel good, but they may take offense and consider that you may be a "trouble maker.")

3. Think about the reason behind the question itself. (Best option if you can think the question through).

4. Consider the source and the nature of the question. (Do you want to work for a company that asks this type of question in an interview?)

There are some exceptions to some personal questions asked, which might be confusing.

Legal Personal Questions

Have you ever been convicted of a crime?
Depending on the type of job you are applying for, this could be critical. The question is usually stated in a more specific manner - "Have you ever been convicted of a felony?"

Can you show proof of your eligibility to work in the United States?
Every new employee, regardless of place of origin, must provide such documentation during the first days on the job.

Can you perform the job's essential functions with or without reasonable accommodation?
This question must be accompanied by a job description covering the essential functions.

The concerns behind these questions are relevant to the job's requirements and performance. As an example, if you have been convicted of embezzlement, you will probably not be considered for a job handling money. The concern is that you had a problem in your past that could be a problem again.

The interviewer wants to know if you can report to work and do the job. Any information that could be enlightening is important, but the interviewer's questions should focus on the job and your qualifications to do it.

By becoming aware of illegal questions, you will be prepared to deal with them if confronted in an interview. Pre-interview thinking and preparation can spare some embarrassing or uncomfortable moments during the interview.

"DO YOU HAVE ANY QUESTIONS?"

Very often at the conclusion of the interview, the interviewer will ask, "Do you have any questions?" The majority of candidates answer this question with a "No." Wrong answer! Don't you want to know something about this company - the interviewer - the opportunity?

The best questions come as a result of the questions they asked you. Listen carefully during the interview, and pick up clues about the company and position from the interviewer.

For example - If one of the questions was about working in a "fast-paced environment," you may want to ask, "What makes this environment hectic? - Quantity or quality?" Find out what the issues are. Is this place inefficient or demanding?

- What are this organization's challenges, problems, opportunities?

- What do you see as future challenges in this industry?

- What changes do you predict for this company in the near future?

- Does this position have a job description? May I have a copy?

- What is morale like on a scale of 1 to 10?

- Why is this position open - new or someone left? If they left - why?

- What are the key skills/qualities necessary to succeed in this job? (your opportunity to let them know you have those skills/qualities)

- What is your management style? (If being interviewed by future supervisor)

- How would you describe the company culture?

- If I asked an employee, "What is the best thing about working for this company, what would he or she say?"

- What types of information/communication systems are in place?

- What would be a typical career path for a person in this position?

- How do you evaluate excellence? How often?

- What type of training programs do you offer new employees?

- What is the next step in the hiring decision?

- How soon would you want the person to start?

Your Values? Fit?

Think about what's important to you in a job. Advancement, challenge, fun, life balance? Remember, you are interviewing them as much as they are interviewing you.

The key is the FIT!

EXERCISE

PREPARE A QUESTION LIST

Would you go on a first date without asking any questions? Begin to think of the interview process as the start of a relationship. Prepare five to ten questions to ask during the interview.

1.

2.

3.

4.

5.

6.

7.

8.

9.

10.

Read Between the Lines

Rose was interviewing for a position as a recruiter when she came across this unusual situation.

The interview had been progressing smoothly until the department head asked if she had any questions. "Yes, I do," she said. "As a potential recruiter, I was wondering how I could convince people they would want to work for this company." The interviewer gave her a rather bland answer, which bothered Rose. She was going to have to sell people on this company if she were to succeed in this role. The interview went on to other subjects, and time passed quickly. At the end of the interview, Rose was asked if she had all of her questions answered. "No, not really," she said. "I still have a question as to why someone would want to work for this company." The department head was hesitant, then replied, "Let's postpone that discussion for another time."

Rose left the interview somewhat dissatisfied and assumed that she had pushed too far with her questions. The next day she received a call from the Human Resources manager with some surprising news. The decision for the position would have to be postponed as the department head who had interviewed her yesterday resigned from the company that morning!

It became clear to Rose why this man had not wanted to sell her on the company.

Sometimes you have to read between the lines. Turn up your intuition!

HOW DO I DRESS FOR THE INTERVIEW?

What image do you want to create? Image is not about being pretty, or having expensive clothing, or even a perfect body. Image is about feeling good about who you are. If you know you look good and are expressing yourself positively, that thought will boost your confidence and in turn affect the way others react to you. The reverse is equally true. If you feel shabby and ill at ease, others will react negatively to you.

Depending on the job and the industry for which you are interviewing, you should dress according to the image that you want to project and what is appropriate. Some candidates are choosing to dress down to project a friendly, more youthful appearance. Each company has its own culture, and what is casual for one company might be unacceptable for another.

If it is possible, go the day before to the place where you will be interviewing and stand outside at lunch time or after work, and watch what the employees leaving the building are wearing. Choose slightly more formal than what you see. After all, you are not one of them yet, and everyone will be aware you are dressing for the interview.

Professional	Ranges from a suit (with tie for men) to a jacket and slacks (no tie). Women can wear slacks/pants suit or skirt as appropriate to the position.
Working casual	No jeans or t-shirts - usually khakis and a collared shirt, jacket or sweater.
Casual	Any type of attire as long as it is tasteful - no gross or slogan t-shirts.
Really casual	Anything goes - no rules as to attire - including the wearing of shoes (the dot-com attitude).

An Interviewer's Story

When I walked into the lobby, I was struck by the starkness of the woman I was about to interview. She was wearing a black suit and stiff white blouse. She had very pale, almost white skin and a lot of bushy, black hair.

She appeared stiff and not the personality type suited for the particular position for which she was applying.

During the interview I asked her, "If I were to ask your co-workers to describe three positive qualities about you, what would they say?" She lit up for the first time during the interview and said, "They'd say I was the life of the office; that I had a great sense of humor; and how much they enjoyed being with me." I sat there with my mouth open. This woman had clearly misrepresented herself by what she had chosen to wear to the interview. She was trying to look very professional, but she went a bit too far. I had made the wrong judgment based on the image she portrayed.

Dress to reflect who you are.
Don't try to be someone else
in an interview.

WHAT IMAGE DO I WANT TO REFLECT?

EXERCISE

What impression do you want to leave?

- What image reflects success to you?

- Consider your favorite news caster or successful person. What does he or she wear?

- Go through magazines or catalogs and look for pictures of people who appear to look successful to you. What are they wearing? Do you want to project that look?

- Make a collage of the pictures of professional people you chose. See if a certain look or pattern begins to develop. Is that your desired look?

THE RULES OF
SALARY NEGOTIATION

THE RULES

> **WARNING:** Take time to consider your options before you begin to negotiate. Salary negotiation can be difficult at best. Once you begin to negotiate an offer you, must be willing to hang in there if your terms are not accepted. The way the negotiation unfolds may set the tone for your future employment with the company.

To say that money is a touchy subject is an understatement. Most people dread the subject, particularly in a job interview. By doing some preparation, some basic research, and following a few rules, you will feel better about dealing with the subject.

Rule #1 – He who mentions a dollar figure first, loses.

Wait until the subject is approached. Then answer that you are open on salary and are looking for an opportunity, or that you would like to postpone that discussion until later in the process. This is a good time to ask what salary range is budgeted for the position. If you are asked what your former salary was, you might state that you would like to hear more about the responsibilities of the job before you compare salaries, or that there were circumstances in your other job that kept your salary below market value. If you are asked what salary you are looking for, depending on where you are in the interviewing process, state that you think it is too early to discuss salary and you would like to hear more about the job before you discuss the particulars of money.

Rule #2 – Never try to negotiate until you have an offer.

You are in a far stronger position to negotiate after you have the offer. Your chances of getting a higher salary improve if the interviewer is convinced you are the right person for the job. This falls somewhere between "They want you" (they're ready to make an offer) and "They got you!" (you've signed on the dotted line, and it is too late to go back and start over).

RULE #3 – Do not accept on-the-spot offers.

Some employers make on-the-spot offers. It is always a good idea to take time to think the offer over. Once you have accepted, it is too late to negotiate any terms of the agreement. If pressed for a decision, tell the employer that you have a personal policy of taking 24 hours to think over major decisions.

RULE #4 – Always get the offer in writing.

Too many people have been burned after negotiating a sweet deal, only to find that when management changes, there is no record of the negotiation. Get it in writing! If you negotiate a change, make sure you get a new offer letter or an addendum memo.

RULE #5 – Keep it friendly.

The tone of the negotiation should never be confrontational. You should be aiming for a win/win situation.

RULE #6 – Consider your position before making deals.

If you cannot settle on a salary, perhaps an early performance review/salary increase can be negotiated. Sometimes you can negotiate on vacation or benefits. The answer is always "NO," unless you ask the question.

RULE #7 – Focus on the base.

It is in your best interest to negotiate the base salary first. Your future raises will be affected by this sum, not to mention Social Security, unemployment, life insurance, etc. The employer's hands are sometimes tied due to internal salary equity. You may be asking for more than some of the current employees are making. Sometimes you will be offered a hiring bonus. Beware, they are usually taxed at a higher rate.

TIP:

SILENCE. It is a powerful tool if used at the right time. Most of us are uncomfortable with silence. If you are offered a dollar amount repeat the amount and then be quiet. Reflect for a moment. Count to five or ten. See what happens!

AFTER THE INTERVIEW

HOW DID YOU DO?

EXERCISE

ASSESSING THE INTERVIEW - YOUR PERFORMANCE

As soon as possible after the interview, you should sit down and write, or use a tape recorder, to get your thoughts out. Just let them flow - dump it all out.

This exercise is for your eyes or ears only!

What is your gut reaction to the process you just went through?

How do you rate your performance? (on a scale of one to five - five being the highest)

What do you think the interviewer(s) thought of you?

What reservations did you hear from the interviewer(s)? spoken or unspoken?

Do you want to work for this company? Why?

What reservations do you have about working there?

Did you address these reservations to your satisfaction?

What looks exciting?

What could you have done differently to be more effective?

What do you still have to find out about the company? job? compensation? benefits?

Let it all go and then walk away from it. Put the writing away or turn off the tape recorder, and forget about the whole thing. Hours later or the next day, pick it up again and read or listen to what you had to say. Are you still feeling the same way? (See exercise Page 84)

IMPORTANT:

After you complete this exercise, it is the time to write your follow-up letter(s) in accordance with your feelings and reactions. **See "Follow-Up Letters" page 86.**

FIT? YOUR NEEDS
THEIR SITUATION AND CULTURE

Complete this exercise after the interview. This part of the equation should be about your values. What's important to you in the job? Does this job fulfill your needs? Is this the right job for you?

What I Want and Need

What They Have to Offer

Doing the exercise is only part of the process. You will now have to step back and do some serious thinking and evaluating.

- Do you want to work for this company?
- Are you picking up vibes that things are not quite right?
- Will you have job satisfaction there?
- Is there a career path?
- Will you have to compromise some of your needs/values?
- Will you fit into the corporate culture?
- Is this the place/job for you?

FOLLOW-UP LETTERS (THANK YOU)

Can Be the Make or Break Point

The "Thank you for the interview" letter is a good way to put yourself in front of the interviewer(s) one more time. Sometimes the follow-up letter can be the tie-breaker between you and another candidate. The follow-up can create goodwill that sets the tone for your future interactions with your potential employer.

You should send the letter within 24 hours of the interview while the experience is still fresh in your mind as well as in the interviewer's.

Make sure the letter is a professional letter that reminds them of the qualities you can bring to the company - your added value. A handwritten letter or note is also acceptable. However, save the printed greeting card for a more appropriate occasion.

Each interviewer has his or her own agenda and should therefore receive a separate letter/Email. This is an opportunity for you to address whatever concern you picked up during the interview - overcome the objection.

Example:

If you were asked, "I see you don't have direct experience in this field," let them know about your transferable skills and how they apply to this job: "I pride myself on the fact that I can adapt and learn quickly. For instance, I transitioned into the sales department at my last company with very little hands-on experience. Yet I was able to make my quotas in record time and even became sales person of the month in the first quarter."

Conclude with your interest in working for the company.
Ask for the job - and use enthusiasm!

This is also a time to let the interviewer(s) know that you are
excited and enthusiastic about the opportunity, and why. What
were the things you liked about the company? The culture?
The product, service, research, cutting-edge technology? The
mission of the company? Why would you want to work for this
company?

This is not a time to talk about the benefits - salary or perks that
will benefit you. This is the time to define what you like about
this particular company and position.

 A Success Story

The interview did not go well for the introverted man.
He had a difficult time expressing himself and talking
about his qualities. His application had been put in the
"reject" pile at the end of the interview.

He really wanted that job and knew he hadn't done well
in the interview. He sat down and wrote a very detailed
letter to the interviewer telling him why he should be
selected for the position and listing the value he could
bring to the company.

When the employer received the letter, he was impressed
and took his resume and the application out and considered it again. The man was called in for a second interview that went much better. He was eventually offered
and accepted the job.

FOLLOW-UP FORMAT EXAMPLE

Dear Interviewer. A separate letter should be sent to each interviewer - addressing interestes or concerns.

Your reaction to the interview. "I left the interview with a million ideas going through my head regarding your company and the challenges of the job." Or, "I came away from the interview feeling confident that I was the solution to your |problem."

Why you want this job. "After talking to you and the other team members, I was impressed with the company's view of future technology." Or, "I have set my sights on working for a company that has the type of culture and mission such as yours - in particular your attitude toward the employees working as a cross-trained team."

What you would bring to the company. Restate your quali-fications - "The added value(s) I would bring to this position would be my ability to solve problems using my past experience and analytical skills, particularly working within tight dead-lines." Or, "I have several reasons to believe I am the solution to your problem..." List the skills and experiences you have that will bring a solution to the job's problems or challenges.

Ask for the "sale." Do you want the job? Let the interviewer know, "I am really excited about the prospect of joining your team and want to be considered as an interested candidate. I know that I would be an excellent fit for the job based on my past experience and what I can bring to the job, and on my future goals."

Sign-off. "I look forward to talking with you further regarding this opportunity." Or, "Thanks again for the interview, I felt very comfortable talking with you and I was impressed with your handling of the interview process."

To Email or Not to E-mail

What about sending the "Thank you" by e-mail?

This is a somewhat controversial issue.

It is ok to send a thank you by e-mail - not politically incorrect. But usually a hard copy sent by regular mail would be the best choice, mainly because the interviewer(s) will have something in hand and tangible to remind them of you and your qualifications.

However, if you get the sense that speed is of importance, then an e-mail would be the fastest way to communicate. One of the problems with e-mail is that it is overused in companies and may not get read. Or if it is read, it may not be remembered unless the reader takes the time to print it out.

You will have to use your judgment based on the situation.

 A Virus Story

E-mail from someone who sent follow-up emails.

"Upon completion of a recent interview, I hurried home and sent out thank you letters to each of the interviewers via e-mail. It has come to my attention three days late, that the letters I attached contained a virus. I am not sure if I should resend a clean copy of the letter and run the risk of closer scrutiny or not send anymore and risk appearing sloppy. Can you provide any guidance in this matter?"

BEWARE OF VIRUSES. THEY CAN STRIKE ANYWHERE AT ANY TIME!

WHAT'S NEXT?
The Most Difficult Part - Waiting

Often at the end of the interview, the interviewer will tell you what the next step is in the decision process. If that does not happen, you may ask, "Could you tell me what the next step is?" You may get a clue as to whether you will be included in the next round. Or, can you expect an offer in the near future?

Don't be surprised if you don't hear back within the time promised.

What if they said they'd call and they haven't? Regardless of what is said, things don't always work out as promised. This is one of the most difficult times in the whole process - the waiting. Be patient. There could be a hundred reasons why it is taking so long.

If one or two days have gone by beyond the time you were told you could expect a call, it would be acceptable to call to find out the status and if you are still in the running for the position. Again, don't be surprised if you leave a message and don't get a return call. This seems to be the norm. If you don't hear back - move on. For whatever reason, you may no longer be under consideration; it is best to go forward and not look back. Every once in a while you might receive a call well after the expected time; at that point it will depend on your status and what has happened in the meantime whether you say, "No, thank you" or move forward. Timing is unpredictable in such dealings. Don't take it personally.

Some applicants have called the company after a rejection and asked for feedback on the interview and qualifications - why they didn't get the job. Most of the time you won't get a true response because of a fear of legal ramifications. The answer most commonly received is, "We found someone who had direct experience." But every once in a while, someone will take the time to tell you what was missing or what you could have done differently. It is worth a phone call if you would like some feedback.

If for some reason, you decide to decline the offer made, follow through with a professional call to say the offer didn't work for you at this time. You never know when another opportunity may come up at the same company. You don't want to burn any bridges.

On-the-Spot Offers

What if they make me an offer and want an immediate decision?

Some employers make on-the-spot offers. It is always a good idea to take time to think the offer over. Once you have accepted, it is too late to negotiate any terms of the agreement. If pressed for a decision, tell the employer that you have a personal policy of taking 24 hours to think over major decisions.

CONCLUSION

PRACTICE, PRACTICE, PRACTICE!

Keep Up the Good Work!

As after any workout you may feel overwhelmed (sore muscles). Don't despair. It will get easier after the groundwork is done. It is very important that you continue to work out. Practice, practice, practice, and become stronger, smoother, and more comfortable.

The goal is not to become over-rehearsed and stiff, but to be prepared and natural. Can you imagine an actor going into a performance without a rehearsal? This is your time to prepare and rehearse.

It is important that you continue to work on your communication skills. If you feel you need one-on-one help, consider working with a professional, or work with a friend or relative who will give you positive and constructive feedback. It is also important that you practice the right way. If you keep practicing, but are repeating mistakes, you will not improve. Think about a tennis or golf swing - it takes a pro to show you the right way.

Maybe you won't get a job offer every time, but preparation will greatly improve your chances and your confidence. Treat each interview as a new learning experience. You may even begin to enjoy the process - some people do!

Get Instant Feedback from a Professional

To schedule your personal consultation, visit my website at www.InterviewCoach.com. After one or more practice sessions with The Interview Coach, whether in-person or phone coaching, your results will improve significantly!

A Success Story

"For the first six months of my job search, I received only slight interest from perspective new employers. Then all of a sudden, in April 2001, I received three requests for interviews all occurring in one week. Oddly enough, when I received my wish for an interview I panicked. I found you through the internet and immediately called. You never pressured me into spending any money or buying your book like some high-pressure sales person. You gave me valuable feedback through mock interviews and suggestions on how to evaluate my strengths and weaknesses."

"After going on the three interviews, I received two offers. By completing the exercises in your book, I was able to make the best career decision for my needs. There was an initial offer of $58,000, but your coaching taught me how to successfully negotiate an additional $7,000, and a performance review after months 6 and 12, which will further increase my salary. There is no way the dollars invested in your program can thank you enough for all the assistance you gave me. Most important to me is that you were extremely patient and professional. Knowing you better now, I realize just how busy your schedule is, but you never rushed me through this process. I would strongly encourage anyone interested in presenting themselves at their best to a potential employer and negotiating the best compensation package, to invest in your program. You have made a friend for life."

Robert Green, "New" General Manager

FORMULA FOR A STELLAR INTERVIEW

1. Prepare
- your personal statement
- your stories (5 or 6 or more)
- your questions to ask

2. Research
- your salary needs
- your worth in your market
- your bottom line

3. Practice
- with a friend
- with a professional*

ABOUT THE AUTHOR

Carole Martin, M.A.

Carole Martin is a professional interviewer, coach, and an expert on the subject of interviewing. In addition to managing her business, www.interviewcoach.com, she has been an interview expert and writer for Monster.com for the past three years.

Her unique background includes over 15 years Human Resources Management experience and a Master's degree in Career Management. She has worked in technical and non-technical industries, in Fortune 500, as well as start up companies.

Martin coaches job seekers on the phone and in person, as well as conducts workshops for people recently laid off from their jobs. She also coaches the MBA students at the Haas School of Business at U.C. Berkeley.

Her education includes a Master's degree in Career Development from John F. Kennedy University in Pleasant Hill, California, where she is an adjunct faculty member teaching interviewing skills to counselors. Her undergraduate degree is in Communications and Public Relations from San Jose State University (achieved at age 40). She has been certified as a Senior Professional in Human Resources (SPHR) by The Human Resources Certification Institute, and has received training at the Coaches Training Institute. She is a certified Behavioral Interviewer.

Martin has been recognized as an interview expert on CNN-FN TV and many radio shows, both in the US and Canada, as well as the BBC. She is frequently quoted in newspapers and magazines - New York Times, LA Times; Men's Health, (May 2002), HR Magazine, Smart Money, Self Magazine, Parents magazine, Employment Management Today, Details, and Employment Review, and Self Magazine.

She is the author of internationally acclaimed, "Boost Your Interview I.Q." (McGraw-Hill), as well as "Interview Fitness Training," which has sold thousands of copies world-wide.

Her life's motto, "It's never too late to make a change," are words she believes in and lives.

OTHER SOURCES

BOOKS

Boost Your Interview IQ, Carole Martin
A virtual interview - 50 questions with 150 possible answers to
test your interviewing ability. Exercises to create your stories -
invaluable for the "Behavioral-based" interview.

Feel the Fear and Do It Anyway, Susan Jeffers, PhD.
For anyone who is feeling powerless and dealing with anxiety.

How to Win Friends and Influence People, Dale Carnegie
My personal favorite. A book that transcends the decades with
current principles of how to interact with other people.

How to Work a Room, Susan RoAne
The ultimate guide to savvy socializing in person
and online - a must in networking.

201 Best Questions to Ask on Your Interview, John Kador
A must for anyone seeking questions to ask in the interview.

The Career Change Resume, Kim Isaacs
A great source of information on making that career
or industry change.

Never Be Late Again, Diana Delonzor
Seven cures for the punctuality challenged.

Find the Bathroom First, Roy Blitzer and J. Reynolds - Rush
Start a new job on the right foot.

SALARY RESEARCH WEBSITES

www.salary.com
Of the salary-type sites I've seen, this is the most straight forward. You can select the job title by geographic region, even down to the zip code if you want, and immediately get a salary range in graph form. There are also good job descriptions.

http://fairway.ecn.purdue.edu/ESCAPE/stats/salaries.html
For engineers.

www.psrinc.com/salary.htm
For MIS Professionals

http://www.wageweb.com

http://www.jobsmart.org
For salary info across multiple fields and geographic locations.

http://www.salaryexpert.com

INTERNET DISCUSSION GROUPS

http://groups.yahoo.com/
You can keyword search this database of e-mail based discussion groups, or browse the categories.

http://www.topica.com/
Topica is a free Internet service that does a great job of allowing you to find, manage, and participate in e-mail lists. E-mail lists are defined as discussion lists, where any subscriber can contribute to the conversation; or newsletters, where one person writes the messages, and the subscribers receive them.

http://www.liszt.com/
This is the most comprehensive source of information on discussion groups. You can keyword search over 90,000 online discussion groups, or browse by subject category. Using the Liszt of Newsgroups, you can search for a newsgroup, or view newsgroups by hierarchy.

http://groups.google.com/googlegroups/deja_announce ment.html
This powerful new Usenet search feature enables Google users to access the wealth of information contained in more than six months of Usenet newsgroup postings and message threads. Once the full Deja Usenet archive is added, users will be able to search and browse more than 500 million archived messages with the speed and efficiency of a Google search